*Leader's Guide
for group study of*

Be Real

Warren W. Wiersbe

Leader's Guide prepared by
DAVID R. DOUGLASS

13   14   15   16   17   18   19   20   Printing/Year   94   93   92

A DIVISION OF SCRIPTURE PRESS PUBLICATIONS INC.
USA   CANADA   ENGLAND

Copyright © 1972, SP Publications, Inc.
World rights reserved. Printed in U.S.A.

A "Briefing" for the Leader

This Leader's Guide is one of a number of guides produced by Scripture Press Publications, Inc., for teachers and leaders of adult study classes in local churches. It is designed for use in

Adult Vacation Bible School classes
Adult and Young People's Sunday School classes
Home Bible Classes
Adult Training Hour classes (before evening church service)
Family devotions (where children are at least 15 years old)

You will find that a careful study of the first six pages of this Guide will greatly increase its value to you.

Page references are to the course textbook unless otherwise noted.

Urge your students, individually, to bring to the class people who have not yet responded to the Gospel. Be careful not to offend or embarrass such visitors needlessly by talking about "the unsaved," etc., or by using "evangelical" expressions that are meaningless to people outside church circles. Don't give any "invitations" unless the Holy Spirit definitely so leads. It is far better to let people know you are available for personal consultation if they want to talk with you. You may want to refer some inquirers to your pastor.

Such teaching methods as buzz groups, brainstorming, circular conversation, and the like are excellent for helping people to participate who find it hard to speak up in public. Once a group enters readily into discussion, however, auxiliary teaching methods become largely unnecessary—provided the leader keeps the discussion on track and prevents its being "monopolized" by aggressive members of the class.

Notify ahead of time the people you will appoint as group leaders and those you will use in role plays, interviews, or other special techniques.

Keep an eye on the clock and be sure to save enough time to close with a summary and an application. The last few minutes of your session are important and should not be hurried.

Bring Bibles — at least N.T.

Planning the Course

Purpose of the Study

This course, "Be Real," is a study of 1 John. As the title implies, Dr. Wiersbe's book emphasizes the truth that *real* living is Christian living—living as God intended man to live. Real living is more than simply being *in* the family of God, it is growing in the Lord—in truth, in obedience, in love.

The textbook has ten chapters and is basically a through-the-book study, though it is not verse by verse. Because John deals with a number of subjects several times each, we combine similar ideas within one lesson, with only casual reference where they occur elsewhere in the epistle. For this reason, it is especially important that you, as teacher of the course, become familiar with the entire textbook—as well as with this *Guide*—before you begin the first session.

For Five Sessions

Each session should be two hours long, with a 10-minute break near the middle. Deal with one of the ten units each half of the session.

For Ten Sessions

Use units 1 through 10 in this *Guide;* omit units 11 and 12.

For Twelve Sessions

Session 1—It's Real (*Text*, chap. 1)
Session 2—Walking and Talking (*Text*, chap. 2)
Session 3—Something Old, Something New (*Text*, chap. 3)
Session 4—The Love God Hates (*Text*, chap. 4)
Session 5—Truth or Consequences (*Text*, chap. 5)
Session 6—The Pretenders (*Text*, chap. 6)
Session 7—Love or Death (*Text*, chap. 7)
Session 8—Getting to the Bottom of Love (*Text*, chap. 8)
Session 9—Love, Honor, and Obey (*Text*, chap. 9)
Session 10—What Do You Know for Sure? (*Text*, chap. 10)
Session 11—Review Lesson
Session 12—Examination (optional)

For Thirteen Sessions

Use the plan for 12 sessions, but spend two periods on one of the chapters, probably Chapter 1, since it introduces the course.

Two Kinds of Lesson Plans

Two kinds of lesson plans are suggested for this course:

    Plan D (Plans are described on next page.)
    Plan W

This chart shows at a glance the circumstances under which to use each plan:

Kinds of Classes	Plan to Use
Classes that meet daily, as in Adult Vacation Bible School Classes that meet weekly in which members do not prepare lessons between sessions	Plan D

Classes that meet weekly, as in
    Adult Training Hour
    Adult Sunday School elective classes
    Home Bible classes
	Plan W

Classes that meet for two hours per session: Devote the first hour to small group study of the textbook as suggested under Plan D. Use the second hour for discussion by the entire class, as suggested under Plan W.	

The suggested plans provide a maximum of participation for members of your class. This is important because—

1. People are usually more interested if they take part.
2. People remember more of what they discuss together than they do of what they are told by a lecturer.
3. People like to help arrive at conclusions and applications. They are more likely to act on truth if they apply it to themselves than if it is applied to them by someone else.

All this presupposes that people are prepared for intelligent discussion. The text of this course readies them for such discussion *even if they do not study between sessions of the class.*

We recommend strongly that you use the chalkboard in your teaching, even if you merely jot down a word or two from time to time to impress a point on the class. When you ask for a number of answers to a question, as in brainstorming, always jot down each answer in capsule form, to keep all ideas before the group. If no chalkboard is available, use a magic marker on large sheets of newsprint over a suitable easel. A printer can supply such paper for you at modest cost.

Encourage class members to bring Bibles or New Testaments to class and use them. It is best if several modern-speech translations are on hand for purposes of comparison.

Lesson Plan D

This plan is especially suited to daily classes, for it is likely that busy class members will not have time to prepare homework. Even if your class meets only once a week, or less frequently, use this plan if you do not intend to assign homework.

At the beginning of the period, divide the class into small study groups of from four to six persons. Don't separate couples. It is not necessary for the same individuals to be grouped together each time the class meets—though if members prefer this, by all means allow them to meet together regularly.

As teacher of the class, lead one of the study groups yourself. Appoint a leader for each of the other groups. If people are reluctant to be leaders, explain that they need not teach and that they need no advance knowledge of the subject. Help your leaders by giving each, a day in advance of the first session, a copy of "Instructions for Group Leaders" (*Guide,* p. 6). You may mimeograph this list so that each leader will have a copy.

Allow the groups and their leaders about half an hour to study the textbook together. Then assemble the entire class. Ask leaders to report questions of unusual interest or that provoked disagreement. Ask the class the questions you want discussed, and allow questions from your students. Be sure to summarize, in closing, what has been learned. Finally, urge each member of the class to make some specific application of the lesson to his life before the next session, as suggested in each unit.

Lesson Plan W

If members of the class use the textbook between sessions, preparing in advance, spend the classtime dealing with the questions asked in the text, urging individuals to share their answers. These answers will provoke further discussion, as will the additional questions provided in the lesson plans in this *Guide.* Be sure to summarize the content of the lesson and to urge personal applications.

If your students prepare between classes, you will have much more time at your disposal, during the teaching session, for discussion and for further instruction.

Additional specific suggestions are given in the lesson plans for each session. Read them carefully, even if you make your own teaching plans. You may get ideas you can use!

Instructions for Study Group Leaders

During the discussion period, ask those in your group to read the sections of the *Text*. The indicated Scriptures should be read. Discuss the questions as they arise, but try to allocate time so that all the *Text* material is covered. Some questions you will, of course, want to refer to the entire class after it reassembles.

After the teacher calls the entire class back into session, be ready to report on questions on which your group disagreed and on contributions you feel are worth sharing.

Here are a few rules for leading discussion:

1. Maintain a relaxed, informal atmosphere. If possible, seat people in a circle or semicircle.

2. Don't call on people by name to participate unless you are quite sure they are willing to do so.

3. Give a person lots of time to answer a question. If necessary, restate the question casually and informally.

4. Acknowledge any contribution, regardless of its merit.

5. Don't correct or otherwise embarrass a person who gives a wrong answer. Thank him; then ask the class, "What do the rest of you think?" or, "Has someone else another view?" People will accept correction best from someone in the group.

6. If some individual monopolizes the discussion, say, "On the next question, let's hear from someone who hasn't spoken yet." If necessary, ask the "monopolizer" privately, after class, to give other people more time to answer questions.

7. If someone goes off on a tangent, wait for him to draw a breath; then say, "Thanks for those interesting comments, Joe. Now let's get back to . . ." and mention the subject under consideration, or ask or restate a question that will bring the discussion back on target.

8. If someone asks a question, allow others in the group to give their answers before you give yours.

SESSION 1

It's Real / *Text, Chapter 1*

Session Goals

1. To become better acquainted with one another. A group always functions more effectively when its members know one another. Such fellowship also makes for better learning.

2. To become familiar with the text, *Be Real,* especially if members have not had opportunity to study it before the course begins.

3. To motivate interest and responsibility for study and other preparation. People learn better when they *want to,* and especially when they participate in the teaching/learning process.

4. To increase and deepen knowledge of God's Word through careful and concerned study of 1 John. To learn from this study more of what "real living" is all about.

Preparation

Survey the entire *Text* and study Chapter 1 carefully. Give special attention also to pages 2-6 of this *Leader's Guide. This is basic.* Underline important passages and make notes as ideas come to you, before you forget them. Encourage your class members to do the same. Become familiar with the entire course, including all units in the *Guide* that you will be using in your study. A thorough knowledge of what is coming up later will enable you to conduct each session more effectively and will help you and your group leaders (if you use them) keep discussion relevant to the subject at hand. If questions are asked that will be considered later in the course, postpone discussion until that time.

Add to your teaching notes for the first session (and for all other sessions as well) material and ideas you think are important and which will be of special help to your class. As teacher, your enthusiasm for the subject, and your personal interest in the persons you teach, will in large measure determine the interest and response of your class.

Provide dittoed or mimeographed instruction sheets (cf. *Guide,* p. 6) for group leaders. Having this material in advance, along with copies of the *Text,* will help them do a much more effective job.

Decide what visual or audio aids you will use this session. If you use the chalkboard suggestions, make sure that board, chalk, and

7

eraser are ready *before* classtime. If you use electrical equipment such as a projector or recorder, make sure you have an extension cord available if needed.

NOTE: We assume that in most classes students will receive their texts at the first session and will have had no opportunity to prepare. The plan suggested for this session is therefore a "D" (daily) plan, which you will probably want to use regardless of the plan you follow during the rest of the course.

[handwritten: Ask how many want the text]

Conducting the Class Session

Start on time. This is especially important for the first session, for two reasons. First, it will set the pattern for the rest of the course. If you begin the first lesson late, members will have less reason for being on time at the others. Those who are punctual will be robbed of time and those who are habitually late will come still later next time. Second, the first session should begin promptly because getting acquainted, explaining the procedure, distributing textbooks, etc., will shorten your study time as much as 10 or 15 minutes.

Begin each session with prayer, asking the Holy Spirit to open hearts and minds, to give understanding, and to apply the truths that are studied. The Holy Spirit is the great Teacher. No teaching, however orthodox and carefully presented, can be truly Christian or spiritual without His control.

If possible, have the class sit in a circle or semicircle. Some who are not used to this idea may feel uncomfortable at first, but the arrangement always makes class members feel more at home. It will also make discussion both easier and more relaxed.

Unless the class is quite large (over 25), remain seated, as much as possible, while you teach. These arrangements help promote a relaxed, informal atmosphere. The most important factor will be your own attitude and manner. Remember that the class is not "yours," but the Lord's, so don't get tense!

Use some means to get the class better acquainted, unless all are well known to each other. If even one person is a stranger, it is a good idea to have each member wear a large-lettered name tag, at least for the first several sessions. It is also helpful to have each

Audio Aid 1

Make a tape recording (or a script to be read in class) of two types of news events—one about some seamy or violent happening, the other about a constructive, helpful, but undramatic act. Ask which of the two better reflects "real life."

person briefly tell something about himself, and perhaps tell what, specifically, he expects to get from this study.

Regardless of the method you use in subsequent sessions, you will probably not want to do much, if any, lecturing this class period. Your first objective should be to help each person become open—to the others present, to you as leader, and to the subject.

Unless the class is very small, divide it, for the duration of the course, into groups of five or six persons each. If most members are willing, ask different people in each group to take turns leading it. Otherwise, use the same group leaders in all sessions. You will probably want to lead one of the groups yourself. Since you will not always use the same number of groups, they will sometimes need to double up or divide. Assign group leaders accordingly.

Begin your study (after getting acquainted, explaining class procedure, and distributing texts) by asking the class to define "real"; cf. Audio Aid 1. (This question is deceptively simple. This word is frequently misused today. Novelists, playwrights, and movie makers often try to justify and promote lurid, violent, or psychotic stories on the basis that they show "real life." The implication is, of course, that the seamy and sinful are somehow more real than are decency, honesty, and normalcy. Actually, good and evil are equally real—contrary to Christian Science, which maintains that only God and His ideals exist. "Real," as it is used in this study, refers to the life God originally created man to have and in which, despite his fallen nature, he can yet participate through trust in Jesus Christ. The real life, therefore, is the Christian life.) After writing proposed definitions on the board and discussing them briefly, divide into three study groups, or three sets of groups, of five or six persons each.

Assign sections for study as follows:

"A" group(s)—section "Fact 1—This Life Is Revealed" (p. 12).

Count off 1-2-3-4-5-1-2-3-etc.

Chalkboard 2

As groups share their findings, write headings on board somewhat as indicated. Feel free to add further detail as needed.

Ask June for chalkboard
" " for 35 or more chairs

THE LIFE THAT IS REAL VITAL FACTS
1— *Revealed*
2— *Experienced*
3— *Shared*
to have fellowship
to have joy
that may not sin
that may not be deceived
that may know are saved

[Margin note: Type these questions for class]

"B" group(s)—section "Fact 2—This Life Is Experienced" (p. 15).
"C" group(s)—section "Fact 3—This Life Is Shared" (p. 18).

Allow 20 minutes for group study and discussion, after which group leaders will report briefly to the entire class. You may want to suggest questions such as the following to group leaders to guide study and to focus discussion:

"A" groups—*What does Jesus' title, the "Word of God," signify? Why is it true that if a man is wrong about Jesus, he is wrong about God? Though the word "Trinity" is not used in the Bible, why is the doctrine of the Trinity so important to the Christian faith?*

[Margin note: I John 3:4-8]

"B" groups—*Did people of Jesus' day have an advantage in that they could physically see, hear, and touch the Lord? What is the difference between being created by God and being born of God? What is the difference between committing and practicing sin? In what ways may a person be a "counterfeit" Christian?*

"C" groups—*What is the difference between changing one's "religion" and changing one's spiritual relationship to God? In what ways does being a Christian solve man's great problem of loneliness? In what ways does being a Christian solve man's greatest problem of sin?*

Since you will probably not have time and will be discussing the subjects in detail later, summarize, but do not discuss, the remaining material. Use the chalkboards as time permits.

[Handwritten note: Assignment next wk 9/19 — Read through all of I John x 1 or 2. Bring Bibles — at least N.T.]

FELLOWSHIP WITH GOD BASES FOR:

HAVING (+)	LOSING (−)
> obedience	> disobedience
> love	> disharmony with other Christians
> truth (light)	> believing lies
[3 great themes in 1 John]	

Chalkboard 3

This chart may be used as a summary of Chapter 1 (cf. *Text*, p. 26) and as a very broad and general outline of 1 John. It can therefore be used either at the beginning or the end of this session.

SESSION 2

Walking and Talking / Text, Chapter 2

Session Goals

Your purpose in this session should be to encourage your members, by God's grace, to live up to a well-known but greatly neglected principle of Scripture—"practice what you preach." In many ways, a well-known but neglected truth is harder to teach effectively—that is, in a way which will produce changed thinking and living—than truth that is not so familiar. This will *not* be an easy session to teach well, but, with the Spirit's blessing, it can be exceptionally rewarding.

Preparation

As with all sessions, your first preparation should be to read the Scripture text carefully, preferably in several translations. Ask the Holy Spirit's guidance in each step of your planning and teaching. Next, read the textbook carefully, making notes and underlining as you do so. This *Leader's Guide* is meant only to supplement the Bible passage and the *Text* and, in fact, cannot be used effectively apart from a thorough study of both. The suggested teaching plans in this *Guide* should be the last thing you study.

Though a relatively short book, 1 John is rich in practical spiritual truths. It is also repetitious, bringing up the same principles or ideas over and over. Unless you plan to have more than 10 sessions, however, you will do well to deal with a theme in only one session, much as is done in the *Text*. Otherwise you will not be able to study all the truths with which this epistle deals. Whether or not you follow the suggested plans, focus each session on one central truth, or on several closely related truths, in the Bible passage. Don't allow yourself to be frustrated by not being able to touch on every facet of the passage. Be content to limit your study to what the Spirit leads you to emphasize for your particular group.

Conducting the Class—Plan W

After prayer, ask, *Why is practicing what we preach so important?* (For ourselves it means faithful, rather than hypocritical, living; for others, it makes our witness to Christ clearer and more believable; cf. Chalkboard 4.)

The main thrust of this passage is negative—walking faithfully by

11

overcoming sin. The positive side—doing what is right and good—is dealt with in later chapters.

How can and should a Christian benefit from the Bible's honest teaching about "sinning saints"? (For one thing, he should be warned against self-righteousness, seeing that even God's greatest men, in themselves, fell far short of His perfect righteousness. He should also be encouraged by realizing when he falls into sin, that God will forgive, bless, and use him, imperfect as he is. He must never, of course, use the "saints' sins" to excuse his own.)

Using Chalkboard 5, point out that the first of the three ways mentioned in the *Text* (p. 31 ff.) for dealing with sin is the wrong, though most common, way. The other two ways are basically two aspects of the same way—trusting Christ to forgive and conquer our sins. It is important that you make clear to your class that John is writing to and about Christians, and therefore *not* about the initial forgiveness and cleansing we have through conversion.

Ask, *What three forms does deceit about our sins take?* (Lying to others, to ourselves, and to God; cf. pp. 32, 33.) *What does a believer stand to lose by not facing his own sins?* (Appreciation and love for the Bible; fellowship with God and other Christians; and his own character; cf. pp. 33-35.)

What is the first step to take in trying to heal a broken relationship with another believer? (To make sure our own attitude and spirit are right both toward God and the other person; p. 34.)

For whom and in what way is Jesus Christ the Advocate? (See p. 36, 2 pars. "Christ is the sacrifice"; cf. Chalkboard 6.) *What does true confession of sin include?* (Admitting the specific sins, judging them as wrong, and renouncing them; cf. p. 38.)

Does a Christian have to sin? (No. No man, especially a Christian, has any excuse for sinning. Though he can never, on his own, over-

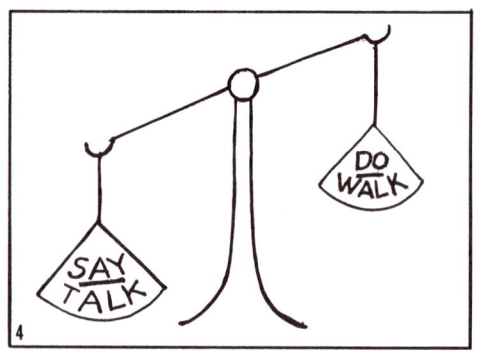

Chalkboard 4
When our words (talk) are "heavy" and our actions (walk) are "light," our witness is left "up in the air."

come sin, he *can* turn to the One who is able to overcome sin for him; cf. p. 40.)

What are the three general motives or reasons for obedience? (Having to, needing to, and wanting to; p. 41.) *Are the first two motives wrong?* (Not necessarily. But, as far as doing what is right is concerned, they are inferior to the last. It is good, for instance, that children attend Sunday School because they *have* to. It is much better that they attend because they understand a *need* for going. It is best, however, that they attend because they *want* to.)

What is the "open secret" of walking in Christ's way? (Abiding in Him. "Incarnation" *by* Christ must precede imitation *of* Him; cf. pp. 43-45.) Close with prayer that your men and women will abide faithfully in Christ so they can both talk *and* walk for Him.

Conducting the Class—Plan D

Divide into study groups and allow 30-40 minutes to read Chapter 2, skimming the first two sections and concentrating on "We Can Conquer Our Sins," pages 40-46. Use chalkboard as needed.

Chalkboard 5
As you discuss the three ways to deal with sin, use this diagram as a visual help. As the author points out, the second two are actually different sides of the same basic way.

THREE WAYS TO DEAL WITH SIN		
1 Cover up — lie to: others, self, God	Submit to God		
	2 Tell God — confess — forsake	3 Defeat sin by abiding in Christ

Chalkboard 6
Satan is a Christian's accuser and Christ a Christian's Advocate before God. You may want to embellish this figure by showing a simplified courtroom scene.

DIVINE TRIBUNAL
JUDGE
(God)

ADVOCATE
DEFENSE
ATTORNEY
Joshua
(Jesus)

ACCUSER
DISTRICT
ATTORNEY
(Satan)

SESSION **3**

Something Old, Something New / Text, Chapter 3

Session Goals

You will need to take special care to keep this session in focus. It is one of several lessons that deal with love. It is partly an introduction to the biblical concept of *agape* love, but it stresses brotherly love—that is, love for fellow Christians. Other aspects of love—for God, self, the world, etc.—should be touched on only as they relate to love for the brethren. Your purpose, therefore, will be to help your adults develop and express greater love for one another, beginning in your own congregation.

Preparation

Several days before class ask several friends (preferably members of the class) to help you make a short recording on the different meanings of "love" in English (Audio Aid 7). Or you may want simply to hand out slips on which the remarks (see below) are written, and have several people read them in turn. Glance briefly at Chapters 4, and 7–9 to see how other aspects of love are treated. Otherwise the class is likely to get off the track into one of these other areas. Note that Chapter 7 also pertains to brotherly love, but from primarily a negative standpoint.

Conducting the Class—Plan W

After prayer, use Audio Aid 7 as an attention-getter. Have members read in turn comments such as the following: "I love my job" (enjoy); "I love your new dress" (find attractive); "Don't you just love homemade apple pie?" (find tasty); "George and Mary are really in love" (are romantically attached); "We love the Martins" (appreciate, have close friendship); "Oh, how I love my little boys" (have devoted affection and concern). After the tape or reading, ask, *What different kinds of "love" are reflected in these remarks you have just heard?* Write answers on the board as they are suggested (possible answers are given above in parenthesis after each statement). *Which of these is nearest to the kind of love talked about in 1 John 2:7-14?* (Most will probably agree on the last one—devoted affection and concern.)

What are the three basic reasons, or imperatives, for Christians to love one another? (See *Text*, p. 48.) *What right did John have for speaking so plainly and boldly about the demands of love?* (In the first place, the Holy Spirit directed him to teach these truths. Secondly, also by the Spirit, he had finally learned to live a life of love, and so was personally qualified to speak about it.) *Had the "Apostle of love" always been loving?* (Hardly. Ask two members to read Mark 3:17 and Luke 9:51-56; cf. p. 48.)

In what ways is Christian brotherly love both old and new? (1 John 2:7, 8; cf. p. 49.) *In what way is Christian love above the Law?* (It fulfills the Law because, by its own nature, it seeks to do God's will and is therefore on a higher level than the Law.) *Is such love ever contrary to God's law?* (Situation ethics and other modern ideas to the contrary, the Bible clearly teaches that God's law and love are never at variance with each other.) Read together Matthew 5:17-19; John 14:21; and 1 John 5:3.

Using Chalkboard 8, ask members to suggest characteristics of an unloving and of a loving nature. Write answers on the board in two columns, then compare these with the characteristics mentioned in Titus 3:3 and 1 Corinthians 13.

What characteristic of agape love sets it above emotion or feeling? (It involves an act of will; cf. p. 53.) *How does this characteristic remove all our excuses for not loving others?* (We can always *will* (decide) and *act* for a person's welfare, regardless of how our feelings or prejudices may incline us; cf. p. 53.)

If Jesus never hated a person (p. 54), *how do you explain His obvious anger on several occasions?* (His anger *with* certain people was based on His hatred *of* what they did. He was angry only when an offense was against His Father, as when He cleansed the Temple, or against others, as when the scribes and Pharisees objected to His healing on the Sabbath. He was never angry, much less hateful, when He Himself was offended.)

Why are love and light (used here as a synonym for God's truth) inseparable? (1 John 2:8-10. They both reflect God's nature, and He is One, indivisible.) *What practical significance does this have?* (A Christian may *know* a great deal about God's light—right doctrine—

Audio Aid 7
Before class begins, hand out numbered slips to five or six class members. After the opening prayer, ask them to read the expressions printed on their slips (see Plan W). They should read with appropriate inflection and emphasis.

without loving his Christian brother, but he cannot be *in* God's light while he hates his brother.)

Why is Christian love not "blind"? (Rather than narrowing or limiting vision, love—because of God's light—sees everything, including sin, more clearly; cf. p. 58. A loving person is aware of faults in others, but he loves in spite of what he sees.)

Ask, *From your own knowledge of Scripture or from reading the Text, how many New Testament "one another" passages that relate to love can you remember?* (See pp. 59, 60 for a partial listing.) *How well does your own life conform to these standards?* (A thought question.) *How can we, as a class and individually, improve our love relation to one another in obedience to these scriptural teachings?* (Ask for specific ways, not generalities. Decide on one way in which, before the course of study ends, your class will help improve brotherly love in your church. Ask each individual to choose at least one specific way he will show greater personal love during this time.)

What are three positive benefits of Christian love? (Better vision and understanding; ② helping, rather than hindering, others; and ③ growth in Christlikeness; cf. p. 62.)

How can Christians generate Christian love? (We can't. It is generated in us by the Spirit when we submit ourselves to His will and use. Cf. p. 64.)

Close with sentence prayers, asking that members pray for specific way for God to improve their love of fellow believers.

Conducting the Class—Plan D

After briefly summarizing pages 47-50 of the *Text*, divide the class into groups to study the three ways Christian brotherly love is new (pp. 50-64). Allow about 25 minutes for study and group discussion. After reassembling, use questions from Plan W.

COMMON CHARACTERISTICS OF	
UNLOVING NATURE	LOVING NATURE
(Titus 3:3)	(1 Cor. 13)
foolish	concern
disobedient	patient
deceived	kind
lustful	humble
envious, etc.	modest
	unselfish, etc.

Chalkboard 8

The characteristics of an unloving or a loving nature, as given in these two Bible passages, are not the only such characteristics, but offer a good general description of the two natures.

SESSION **4**

The Love God Hates / Text, Chapter 4

Session Goals
The theme of this session is worldliness and its relation to a Christian. You will be stressing a negative side of godliness—overcoming the world. Your purpose will be to help your men and women, in practice as well as in theory, to hate worldliness as God hates it.

Preparation
As you plan this session, ask the Holy Spirit to convict you of worldly attitudes and practices in your own life and to give you strength to overcome them. This would be your best possible preparation, for the best teacher of a truth is one who has applied the truth in his own life. Make the "coin of righteousness" (or ask a class member to make it) according to instructions in Visual Aid 9.

Conducting the Class—Plan W
Open with prayer and then ask the class to form a definition of worldliness. Jot down ideas on the board as they are suggested and then combine into a single, clear definition as best you can. Do not discuss it at length at this time. Next, display the "coin of righteousness" (see Visual Aid 9), pointing out that love of good and hatred of evil are essentially two ways of saying the same thing. Ask, *Is hatred always wrong? Why?* (No; in fact it is inescapable. If you truly love something, you cannot keep from hating whatever is against it; cf. Matt. 6:24; *Text*, p. 65.)

Just as there is a right kind of hate, there is also a wrong kind of love. *What is the "love that God hates"?* (Love of the world, especially in His children.)

Divide the class, at this time, into four buzz groups (or sets of groups). Ask each group to discuss one of the four reasons Christians have for not loving the world (see the subheads in Chapter 4 of the

---

Visual Aid 9

From a piece of posterboard (gold or silver, if possible), cut two circles (10 to 18 inches in diameter) and glue back to back. Use one circle if board is double-faced. Mark to indicate milled edges and print on either side "loves good" and "hates evil." You may print "RIGHTEOUSNESS" around border on both sides.

17

Text). Allow about 10 minutes for group discussion and then reassemble. Use the following questions and comments to help direct class discussion as reports from the groups are given.

1 Because of What the World Is. *What different meanings are found in Scripture for "world"?* (See p. 66.) *Which meaning is in view in 1 John 2:12-17?* (The world as system of ideas, standards, and allegiance.) *What are some of the characteristics of this system?* (It is directed by Satan, its prince; it opposes God; all unbelievers and carnal believers are its servants; it is not a Christian's natural habitat or environment; cf. pp. 66, 67; Chalkboard 10.)

2 Because of What the World Does to Us. *Why is worldliness "not so much a matter of activity as of attitude"?* (p. 68. It is primarily a "heart condition," involving desires, motives, and intentions. It can be strong even when it is not expressed in action.) At this time, compare your class's definition of worldliness with the one suggested by Dr. Wiersbe (p. 69). Ask, *What is the relation of worldliness to moral sins?* (All moral sins are worldly, but not all worldliness involves moral sin. Even things quite good in themselves can become worldly for *us* because of the way we use or misuse them. Cf. pp. 69, 70, especially the story of the student preacher.) *What characteristic do the three devices of the world (1 John 2:16) have in common?* (Self-gratification/self-interest; cf. pp. 70-73.) *Why is "lust of the eyes" perhaps the most dangerous of these "devices"?* (Because it is basically an inner sin, and is therefore easier to justify and to hide from others. It includes what may be called "vicarious sinning"—enjoying thinking, hearing, or reading about sins that we probably would never commit actively.) *What common expressions typify "pride of life"?* ("Keeping up with the Joneses," "conspicuous consumption," "You only go around once," and the like.) *Into which of the three devices is it perhaps easiest for Christians to fall?* (The last,

SURVIVAL IN AN ALIEN ATMOSPHERE	
astronauts in space	Christians in the world
– no air	– ungodly
– no water	– unjust
– no food	– unloving
– no gravity	– untruthful

Chalkboard 10
Your adults are familiar with the vital, intricate, and expensive support systems necessary to maintain men in space. Christ, through His Spirit and Word, is the Christian's "support system."

pride of life, since its manifestations often seem innocent.)

3 Because of What a Christian Is. This reason consists of only one basic truth: a Christian is a child of God and therefore has no business flirting with a system that is the enemy of his Father. *What are the three degrees of maturity described in 1 John 2:13, 14?* (Childhood, youth, adulthood.) *In which stage is a Christian more vulnerable to the world?* (The first, just as a child is more susceptible to physical dangers.) *In what other ways is spiritual maturity like mental?* (Advance in years does not guarantee advance in maturity. Spiritual retardation is all too common; cf. p. 76.)

4 Because of Where the World Is Going. *Why does godliness (the opposite of worldliness) require more than avoiding evil and doing good?* (Godliness requires our following God's perfect will in everything. He may lead us away from many things that are good in themselves. Cf. p. 79.) *By what means can a Christian know God's will?* (By surrender to the Lord, study of His Word, circumstances, and the direct leading of the Holy Spirit; cf. pp. 80-82.)

Close with prayer that you will learn to hate the world more by loving God more.

Conducting the Class—Plan D

Divide into four groups as described in Plan W, but allow 25 minutes for group study and discussion before coming back together. Whether or not you use Visual Aid 9, stress the truth of the two "sides" of righteousness.

Chalkboard 11
If you have time, read Gen. 13:5-13; 14:8-14; and chap. 19, tracing Lot's spiritual descent on the board as you read about each downward step.

```
LOT'S SPIRITUAL DECLINE
         (GENESIS)
  looked toward Sodom
  pitched tent toward Sodom
  moved into Sodom
  socialized with Sodomites
  suffered because of Sodomites
  lost family respect
  lost self-respect
```

SESSION **5**

Truth or Consequences / Text, Chapter 5

Session Goals
This session deals with false teachers and teaching a Christian's attitude toward them. Stress the vital importance of right belief in relation to right living. Right belief (truth) is the root and right living the fruit of the Christian life. Depending on the makeup of your class, you may want to spend considerable time discussing the popular notion that what a person believes isn't so important as long as his "heart is right," that is, he is sincere.

Preparation
Read Chapter 5 in the *Text* several times—after you are thoroughly familiar with the Scripture passage (1 John 2:18-29; 4:1-6). Then study the suggestions in this *Guide,* underlining and making notes in each case. Unless most of your members are already well-informed about end-time Bible teaching, plan to cover in detail the section on "last time" and "antichrist" (*Text,* pp. 84-86). Have a road map marked and ready to use in class (Visual Aid 12).

Conducting the Class—Plan W
Open with prayer. Then hold up the map before your class and ask, *Suppose three travelers each took one of the three routes marked on this map* (cf. Visual Aid 12). *They all sincerely think that the route they chose will get them to . . . .* (the destination you select). *Of what value is their sincerity as far as actually reaching . . . . is concerned?* (Obvious answer is "None.") If you have unbelievers in your class, ask, *Of what value is religious sincerity in getting a person to heaven if it is not based on God's truth?* (Again, answer is obviously "None.") The same type of question could be asked of Christians in relation to moral standards, prejudices, rewards, the Second Coming, and the like. Sincere beliefs about these areas are of value only if they are *right* beliefs.

If your class members are well-informed about end-time prophecy, simply comment briefly on what Dr. Wiersbe says about the "last time" and "antichrist." Otherwise, using Chalkboard 13, brainstorm members for their ideas about these two terms. (Brainstorming is simply asking the class to give ideas freely, without argument, comment, or discussion. Don't show alarm over ideas that are "far out" or sound foolish. Your purpose is to find out what folks' thinking *is*. Where it is wrong or hazy, the rest of the class session, hopefully, will bring clarification. Remember, if we were already perfect in our knowledge, understanding, and obedience, we wouldn't need such studies as this! A good first step in learning the truth often is to get wrong ideas out in the open.) As you discuss the two great opposing forces in the universe—God/Satan, truth/falsehood, etc. (*Text*, p. 84)—be sure your class understands that these are not *equal* powers, nor is the outcome of their conflict uncertain. Satan is a fallen creature of God; the Lord has already set the day for the adversary's destruction.

As you discuss the marks of false teachers (*Text*, pp. 86-97), point out that *describing* them is nearly always easier than *identifying* them. As important as it is to recognize genuine false doctrines and attitudes, it is also important *not* to brand everyone who disagrees with us as being a heretic or apostate.

What kind of departure from fellowship is mentioned in 1 John 2:19 and discussed under section 1 in the Text (pp. 86-89)? (Leaving the fellowship of true believers because one cannot tolerate biblical doctrine and spiritual standards of living. Disagreement is over primary Bible truth, not over areas such as mode of baptism, about which evangelical Christians have long had differences of interpretation.)

Deniers of the faith (section 2) are those who are mistaken about *who Jesus is*—the divine Son of God who became a man. Apart from this basic truth, all other doctrines—the Virgin Birth, Christ's atonement for our sins, the Resurrection, etc.—would be meaningless. Unless Jesus *is* who the Bible says He is, He could not have *done* all the things the Bible claims He did and continues to do. *What is infinitely*

Visual Aid 12
On a road map, circle with a felt-tip pen the city where you are and another city some distance away. Draw one line (in a color easily seen) following the normal route between the two cities. Draw two other lines from your city leading in directions *away from* the other city. Use as indicated in Plan W.

more important than RECOGNIZING *Jesus as the Saviour of men?* (Being *related* to Him as our own Saviour; cf. *Text,* p. 90, par., "To confess that.")

As discussed in section 3, *Why do you suppose Satan is more concerned about deceiving Christians than non-Christians?* (Non-Christians are already deceived and belong to Satan. Satan wants to weaken Christ's Church and even take away believers—if that were possible.) *Why is Satan primarily a "counterfeiter"?* (For one thing, he is blinded to the truth and is uncreative. Truth is necessary for real creativity. Second, it is easier to deceive with what looks like the real thing than with what is obviously a fake. Cf. *Text,* pp. 92-94. Counterfeit faith is discussed further next session.)

What are a Christian's main protections against false teachers and their perverse ideas? (Knowledge of God's Word and the interpreting and leading of the Holy Spirit; *Text,* pp. 93, 94.) *Why is a balanced understanding of* all *God's Word so critical?* (Partial truth is often more dangerous than outright falsehood. Most cults are based on a few scriptural truths—but they neglect and even deny the rest of Scripture. Cf. *Text,* p. 93.)

If time allows, review the eight "abides" in 1 John 2. You will probably have little time to study the "bridge" passage (2:28, 29; *Text,* pp. 97-100) between *fellowship* and *sonship.* Ask someone in advance to prepare a brief summary of this material, or do so yourself.

Conducting the Class—Plan D

Assign sections of the *Text* for group study according to what you want to emphasize (see "Session Goals" and "Preparation"). Both Visual Aid 12 and Chalkboard 13 will be helpful in stimulating and directing discussion.

"LAST TIME"	"ANTICHRIST(S)"
when?	who is it?
how come about?	who are they?
who wins?	how identify?
what happens?	will Christians contend with?

Chalkboard 13

As you brainstorm members for ideas about the two subjects, use the questions listed in the figure as guides. Simply list, and do not discuss or comment on, at this time.

SESSION 6

The Pretenders / *Text, Chapter 6*

Session Goals

Since this chapter concentrates on the two types of people in God's sight—His children and Satan's children—you will have excellent opportunity for an evangelistic thrust. If most or all of your class members are Christians, stress living completely in the new nature we have in Christ.

Preparation

Study carefully Chapter 6 in the *Text*, keeping in mind the particular needs of your class. You may want to suggest indicated Scripture passages outside 1 John for special study, again depending on your emphasis. For Visual Aid 14, have a Bible, copies of *Science and Health*, the *Watchtower*, *Plain Truth* magazine, the *Koran*, etc., ready for display. If you cannot find actual copies of such works, letter these titles on separate sheets of paper (preferably colored) and use as "jackets" over other books. Most public libraries, however, will have numerous titles of cult and other non-Christian works.

Conducting the Class—Plan W

After prayer, ask, *Why would merely studying dozens, even hundreds, of counterfeit bills not qualify a person to distinguish between genuine and spurious currency?* (Without the genuine article to judge by, there is no way to distinguish between real and counterfeit currency; cf. *Text*, p. 101.) *What is the only way, therefore, to learn how to distinguish between true and false religious ideas and practices?* (Thorough knowledge of God's Word, the only reliable standard of spiritual truth.) Referring to Visual Aid 14, comment to the effect that study of cultic, pagan, or modernistic literature alone will only confuse a person who has little or no knowledge of Scripture.

According to 1 John 3:10, what are two basic characteristics that distinguish true believers from pretenders? (True Christians practice righteousness and love each other; cf. *Text*, p. 101.) *Besides helping us tell true from false believers, of what additional value is this verse to Christians?* (It suggests that the *degree* of our practicing righteousness and loving fellow Christians is an indication of how faithfully we are living for Christ.)

23

2. *What is the critical difference between the kinds of sin mentioned in 1 John 1:8, 9 and that described in 3:6, 9?* (As most modern translations make clear, the first passage is speaking of practiced, habitual sin; the second pertains to occasional, nonhabitual sin; cf. *Text,* pp. 102, 103.) *To which kind does a Christian's nature restrict him?* (The latter. Even this limited form of sin, of course, is possible only when we allow the old nature to assert itself over the new.)

As you discuss the three reasons for living a holy life, use Chalkboard 15 as an outline guide. These reasons apply only to Christians, since only they have the potential for holy living. God's love for His children is so absolutely basic that, in a real sense, it covers the other two reasons, especially the second. Because of His great love, the Father sent His Son to die for us and the Son willingly laid down His life. Because of God's continuing love, He also gives us His very Spirit to indwell and strengthen us.

In light of what great future event is holy living frequently admonished in the New Testament? (The second coming of the Lord Jesus Christ; 1 John 3:2, 3; cf. 2:28; Phil. 3:20, 21; *Text,* p. 104.)

What three states of spiritual life are mentioned in 1 John 3:1-3? (What we *are*—God's children, v. 1; what we *shall be*—like Christ, v. 2; what we *should be*—pure, v. 3.) *What should our attitude be in regard to these wonderful truths?* (Could be answered in many ways, but could be put: *thankful* for what we are, *hopeful* for what we shall be, and *careful* for what we should be.)

How and why is sin in a Christian worse than sin in an unbeliever? (A Christian's sin is against His Father as well as His Creator; he sins against love as well as against law; and he sins out of greater light, responsibility, and power to resist; cf. *Text,* p. 105.)

What two great works that Jesus accomplished on the cross are mentioned in 1 John 3:4-8? (His taking away our sins and His destruction of the devil's works.) *What is the relation of sin to rebellion against God?* (They are essentially the same. Sin not only leads to but results from rebellion against God and His law. Sins—that is, specific acts of evil—are simply the manifestation of the basic nature and spirit of sin/rebellion/lawlessness; cf. *Text,* p. 107.) *How do our union and communion with Christ relate to our sin?* (Our union with

Visual Aid 14
From your public library or other source, collect books, pamphlets, or magazines published by a number of cults or non-Christian religions. Display them on a table in front of the classroom with an open Bible in front of the other material.

Christ by the new birth saves us from the penalty of sin; our communion with Christ through continuing fellowship with Him keeps us from falling into sins; cf. 3:3, 6, 9; *Text*, pp. 107, 108.)

Of what special importance for believers is Christ's destruction of the devil's works? (First He has conquered Satan's power of death over sinners who believe in Him. Second, as we rely on His Holy Spirit, He continues to protect us from Satan's luring us back into sin.)

Put briefly, what are the distinctive meanings of "justification," "sanctification," and "regeneration"? (See *Text*, p. 111, par., "Justification means.") *What common needs do the old and new spiritual natures have?* (They both need feeding, cleansing/healing, and exercise; cf. *Text*, pp. 112-114.)

Conclude this session by writing the checklist of five questions (*Text*, pp. 117, 118) on the board. As heads are bowed, read the questions aloud and ask members to consider before God how they should answer each. Close with prayer that the Holy Spirit will work in each life the ministry needed.

Conducting the Class—Plan D

If you plan an evangelistic emphasis, concentrate on section 2 of the chapter—"God the Son Died for Us" (*Text*, pp. 105 ff.) Otherwise stress sections 1 and 3. Assign group study accordingly and use appropriate help from Plan W.

Chalkboard 15

Since Chapter 6 is rather involved, a general outline, such as given here, should prove helpful. Do not put on board all at one time, but add segments as they are discussed.

> *Father loves us* (3:1-3)
> what we-are
> — shall be
> — should be
> *Son died for us* (3:4-8)
> — take away our sin
> — destroy devil's works
> *Holy Spirit lives in us* (3:9, 10)
> we need — feeding
> — cleansing/healing
> — exercise

25

SESSION 7

Love or Death / Text, Chapter 7

Session Goals

The theme of this chapter is human relationships, dealt with on four levels—murder, hate, indifference, and love. They are presented in 1 John and in the *Text* in order of increasing desirability. You will consequently want to stress murder the least and love the most. <u>Where true Christian love exists, the other three cannot.</u>

Preparation

After reading the Scripture passage, 1 John 3:11-24, several times in at least two different versions, pray that the Lord will strengthen *your* love—beginning with your relationship to your class members. Besides considering your teaching of the group a ministry of love—which hopefully it is—ask to be guided to specific and individual ways you can express love to members, in and outside of class. Study the *Text* and *Guide* thoroughly, looking up and making notes on *all* Scripture passages used. You will not have time to discuss all of them—for your main study is in 1 John—but select for emphasis a few of the other Scriptures that give additional teaching on the truths being studied. The Bible is still its own best commentary.

Conducting the Class—Plan W

After prayer, have the class read together Genesis 4:1-8 and Hebrews 11:4. Using Chalkboard 16, compare the sacrifices of Cain and of Abel. The three most important truths to emphasize are: God was not arbitrary in refusing Cain's sacrifice, since Cain had not done well (Gen. 4:7)—had obviously disobeyed God; Abel's sacrifice was accepted because it was offered in faith (Heb. 11:4), in obedience to God; Cain's disobedience of God and hatred of his brother resulted in murder.

Ask — *What is the primary difference between hatred and murder?* (Hatred is an inner attitude, murder an outward act; cf. *Text*, p. 123, par., "At this point.") *During any period of human history, why have there been many more murderers—as far as intent is concerned—than actual murders committed?* (Simply because countless people have refrained from committing the act *only* for fear of punishment, or from cowardice; cf. *Text,* p. 124.) *In what ways are hatred and murder, lust and adultery, and covetousness and stealing alike?* (The former attitude, in each case, leads to the latter act if unchecked, and is actually a form of the latter; cf. Matt. 5:21, 22, 27, 28; *Text,* pp. 124, 125; Chalkboard 17.) *Who suffers the most from lust, hatred, or covetousness—assuming they are not expressed in action?* (The persons having these sinful attitudes; cf. *Text,* p. 125, par., "Hatred does.")

Why is indifference to the needs of others such a common and dangerous sin, even among Christians? (It *seems* to be "neutral" and innocent, since no conscious ill will or overt act is involved.) *How neutral or innocent is indifference, however, in light of 1 John 3:16, 17?* (It is definitely sinful. No person can escape being aware of *some* needs in those around him, and for a Christian to do nothing to meet such needs is a denial of the love of God which he is called to manifest; cf. James 4:17.)

What does willingness to "lay down our lives for the brethren" (1 John 3:16) mean? (Willingness to give of ourselves to whatever extent is required.) *How does the parable of the Good Samaritan relate to this truth?* (We should be concerned about *being* a neighbor, giving ourselves to others; cf. *Text,* p. 127.)

In what way is "in word" the opposite of "in deed," and "in tongue" the opposite of "in truth"? (When we speak of doing good, but take no action, we prove that our main concern is to help ourselves by making a good impression, rather than to help others; cf. *Text,* pp. 129, 130, 4 pars., "True Christian love.")

In what way are the costs of salvation and of discipleship alike, and in what way are they different? (Both are willingly paid because of love; but Jesus alone paid the cost of salvation, whereas each Christian pays the cost of his own discipleship.) *What are some of the*

Chalkboard 16
Cain's murder of Abel resulted from more than a hateful, jealous flare-up. And these brothers were different in many other areas besides the occupational.

AREAS OF COMPARISON	CAIN	ABEL
sacrifice	grain	animal
trusted in	self	God
served	Satan	God
motive	pride	faith
outcome	murder (death)	salvation (life)

27

rewards of costly discipleship—loving in "deed" and "truth"? (*Assurance* of one's relationship with God, 1 John 3:19, 20; *answered prayer* because of being in God's will, vv. 21, 22; and *abiding* in fellowship with Christ by His Spirit, vv. 23, 24, cf. *Text,* pp. 130-134; Chalkboard 18.)

ASK. *In what way are human relationships a matter of "love or death"?* (God's love, through His Son, brings life, and our love is evidence that we have received the life so offered; therefore having no love means having no life; cf. *Text.* p. 136.)

Conducting the Class—Plan D

Allow your groups a good share of the time—perhaps 30 minutes—for study. Ask them to give special attention to pp. 119, 120 and 126-136 in the *Text* and to look up and discuss the Scripture references given. As always, consult Plan W for helpful ideas.

INTENT (INNER)	ACTION (OUTER)
hatred	murder
lust	adultery
covetousness	stealing

17

Chalkboard 17
As you discuss the relation of intent and action, read the relevant passages from Matthew 5 and chart the relationships as indicated.

REWARDS FOR LOVING IN DEED/TRUTH
assurance (3:19, 20) because right with brother
answered prayer (3:21, 22) because right with God
abiding (3:23, 24) because close to God

18

Chalkboard 18
Rewards for faithful living in the Lord are not *all* reserved for heaven. List temporal rewards and reasons as they are discussed.

SESSION **8**

Getting to the Bottom of Love / *Text, Chapter 8*

Session Goals

As Dr. Wiersbe points out, this is the third chapter that centers on love. This session focuses first of all on God—His *nature* of love and His *works* of love for, in, and through His children. These are foundations on which *our* love is to be built. Your goal should be to help your adults grow in their personal relationship with God and in their willingness both to receive and to manifest His love.

Preparation

As you study the Scripture passage and the *Text,* keep in mind the new truths emphasized here. Review your notes on Sessions 3 and 7, and then take special care to develop this session in a way that will build upon, but not "rehash," what you covered previously.

Chapter 3 pertained largely to the *meaning* of Christian love and Chapter 7 to the *place* of Christian love as the highest and only acceptable form of personal relationship. This session goes still deeper and presents the reasons or bases—the "why"—of Christian love.

Find a magnetic compass to use in class with Visual Aid 19. If you cannot locate a real one, draw a facsimile of a compass on a piece of poster board.

Conducting the Class—Plan W

Open with prayer. Holding up the compass, or your drawn facsimile (Visual Aid 19), ask, *What is the purpose of a compass?* (To indicate accurate direction by pointing north.) *Does a compass determine which is north?* (No, it only points in that direction.) *How is a Christian's love relationship to God here illustrated?* (When we are rightly related to Him, our love points to, but does not determine, God's love, as a compass needle responds to the earth's magnetic field; cf. *Text,* p. 138.)

Visual Aid 19
If possible, bring a magnetic compass to class. If you can't find the real thing, draw a facsimile of a compass on a piece of poster board.

29

What are the three divine "foundation stones" on which John builds his admonition for Christians to love one another? (God *is* love; God *acted in love* by sending His Son to redeem man; God *continues* to *show His love* by abiding in those who have trusted His Son; cf. pp. 138, 141, 145.)

What common misinterpretations are made of the biblical teaching that God is love? (Many people seem to think that God is *only* love, and they disregard His holiness, justice, sovereignty, etc. Many also think that love defines God, whereas the opposite is true. Cf. pp. 139, 140.) *What great danger lies in the idea that love defines God?* (Deciding what God is like on the basis of our preconceived, personal, and unbiblical concepts of love.)

ASK *What does the Bible expression, "knowing God," mean?* (To have met God and to have a personal relationship with Him through trust in His Son. The term is a synonym for being His child, for being saved, etc.; cf. p. 140.) *What is the measure of a Christian's love?* (His Christlikeness, since Christ, being God, *is* love; 1 John 4:8, 16; cf. pp. 140, 141.)

Do This Ask class members to read silently 1 John 4:9-11; Rom. 3:23-25; 5:6-11. After they have read these passages ask, *Which more greatly manifested God's love—Jesus' birth and incarnation or His death and resurrection?* (They are, of course, inseparable in God's plan, but without Christ's death and resurrection men would have been left in their sins, with no possibility of salvation. If Jesus had lived as only a perfect Man among men, the highest standard of righteousness would have been set before us but we would have had no means of achieving it. Jesus' incarnation, without His atoning death and resurrection, would have been a mockery of men. ASK *In what two basic ways was God's sending His Son to redeem men (1 John 4:10) evidence of His great love?* (In the great *cost* to God and the great *benefit* to men; cf.

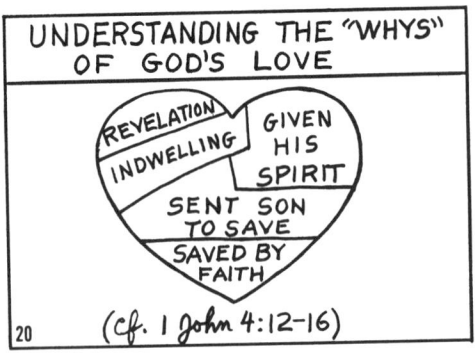

Chalkboard 20

Understanding some of the "whys" of the working of God's love helps us see His overall plan of redemption more completely and in better perspective. The placement and size of the segments in the figure have no logical or theological significance.

Ask
p. 143.) *Why must our Christian love, to be truly spiritual and effective, involve our minds and wills?* (Without understanding and action, love is likely to be "sentiment without responsibility." Cf. p. 144, par.,"We should remember.")

Of what practical help is an understanding of the "why" of God's loving acts? (We can serve Him more intelligently and with greater appreciation when we can "read the script" and see the pieces of the divine "puzzle" together in one picture. Cf. pp. 145, 146; Chalkboard 20.)

In what ways is God's love "incarnated" (living in us) today? (See p. 149, 2 pars.,"Three different witnesses.") *How does love prove itself to be alive?* (By growing in believers who allow it to take root within them, and also by stimulating growth in every other spiritual virtue. See p. 150; Chalkboard 21.)

How is love a "commandment," a "privilege," and a "consequence"? (See Text, p. 151, par., "God is love.") *Why must love determine not only what we do but how we do it?* (If our action doesn't match our words, it will contradict them; cf. story of Helen and her devotions, p. 152.) *When can being "nice" not be loving?* (When our motive is self-interest; cf. p. 153.)

※ Close with sentence prayers from class members asking God's help in their receiving, sharing, and showing His love.

Conducting the Class—Plan D

You may want to spend a bit more time than usual studying the Text. After reassembling, use chalkboards and questions, from Plan W, as needed.

Chalkboard 21

A maturing Christian grows in each of the major areas of spiritual life— love, truth, faith, and obedience. As in Figure 20, the arrangement of these areas in the diagram has no particular significance.

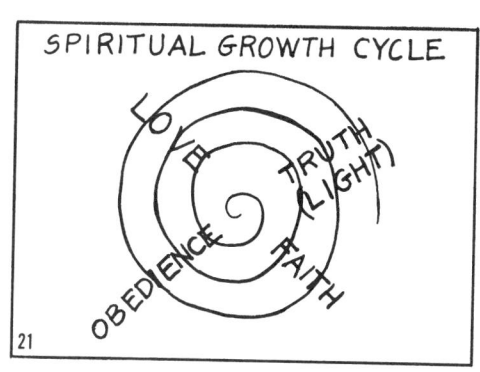

SESSION 9

Love, Honor, and Obey / Text, Chapter 9

Session Goals
Just as faith without works is dead, love without obedience is dead. Love is on a higher level than law, but it is never contrary to law (that is, God's law). It is impossible to love God and not obey Him, John emphasizes in this session's passage. Your obvious purpose will be to help your members, motivated by their love for the Lord, grow in their obedience to His will.

Preparation
Study 1 John 4:17—5:5 in several translations, as well as related Scripture passages suggested in the *Text*. Take a brief inventory of your own life to determine how well you are growing in God's love according to the four evidences discussed in this lesson—especially in the area of joyful obedience. At the previous class session, ask a member to prepare a report on Psalm 119. He is to find all the synonyms for "Law" (Word, statutes, etc.), for "love" (respect, delight, etc.), and for "obey" (keep, observe, etc.). He should be prepared to write these terms on the chalkboard at the appropriate time (see Plan W). For use with Visual Aid 22, bring to class two checks, one blank, the other filled out. Pray that the Holy Spirit will strengthen you and your class members in living the love you have as God's children.

Conducting the Class—Plan W
Open with prayer. Ask, *What is the meaning of "perfect" love (Authorized Version) in 1 John 4:17?* (It does not mean absolute or flawless, such as is God's love, but rather "complete" or "mature." It is love as God intends it to be in His children; cf. *Text*, p. 156.)

Divide the class into four study/buzz groups (four sets of groups if class is large) and assign topics as follows:
- Confidence—1 John 4:17-19; *Text*, pp. 156-160.
- Honesty—4:20, 21; pp. 160-163.
- Joyful obedience—5:1-3; pp. 163-166.
- Victory—5:4, 5; pp. 166-171.

Ask each group to look for and record ways in which these four characteristics of Christian living depend upon and are the natural consequences of love—God's love for us, ours for Him, and/or ours for others. After coming back together in about 10 minutes, use the following questions and suggestions to discuss each section in turn. Allocate available time so that each area is dealt with.

Confidence *Fear in a Christian is an evidence of what?* (Incomplete love; 1 John 4:18; p. 157.) *Why is a Christian's fear both unnecessary and foolish?* (Everything of ultimate importance is secured for him in Christ.) *How does our perfected love in Christ guarantee "freedom of speech" ("boldness," AV) in the day of judgment?* (See 1 John 4:17; p. 157, par.,"The word 'boldness.' ") *What kind of fear does love include?* (Reverential fear of God; cf. p. 159. True love is bold but respectful.) *What is the secret of "holy boldness" or confidence?* (Realization of—understanding and relying upon—the truth that, because we now belong to Christ, God regards us as He does His own Son; 4:17; cf. p. 159.)

Honesty *Why do fear and pretense go together?* (Fear of what others would think or do if they knew us as we really are causes us to pretend to be better than we are—to put on a pious mask or front; cf. p. 160.) *Why is such pretense unnecessary for a Christian?* (Because in spite of his faults and imperfections, he is eternally accepted by God in Christ. His faults and sins should cause shame and desire for forgiveness, but not fear or pretense.) *Why do confidence and honesty go together?* (See previous answer.) *Why is hypocrisy so debilitating?* (Hypocrisy is a form of lying, and a liar must constantly be on his guard lest he trip himself up by some inadvertent inconsistency or contradiction.) *Why is honesty invigorating?* (It allows us freely to use our energy in serving the Lord, without the tension and wasted energy of trying to keep up a front; cf. p. 162.)

Joyful obedience *If God's commandments are not burdensome (5:3), why do many Christians find them so difficult to keep?* (Because they try to obey in their own power rather than in God's. Obedience is *for* us but, in its deepest sense, it not *by* us.) *Is dutiful obedience wrong?* (It is not so much wrong as immature and incomplete. It is better than disobedience, but because it relies primarily on self, it can never be truly successful or joyful; cf. p. 163.) *What is the*

Visual Aid 22

For use when discussing our claiming of God's promises, bring to class a blank check and one that is filled out and signed but not endorsed. Comment that money in a checking account is useless until a check is drawn on the account. Similarly, a check is useless until it is endorsed.

secret of joyful obedience? (Love of God and reliance on His grace and power; 5:2, 3; cf. p. 165.) At this time ask the person who prepared the report on Psalm 119 to share his findings with the class (see Preparation).

Victory Victory that overcomes depends on faith, 5:4. *Are all Christians victorious, then?* (They are all victorious over sin and death by their trust in Christ as Saviour.) *In what ways may Christians not be victorious?* (In daily living. Daily victories require daily faith; cf. pp. 166, 167.) *What kind of faith is not victorious?* (Faith in anything or anyone but Jesus Christ; v. 5; p. 168.)

What is the greatest barrier to victorious living? (Sin—which erodes confidence, honesty, and joyful obedience as well as victory; cf. p. 169.) *What is probably the next greatest hindrance to victorious living?* (Failure to claim God's promises, accept His help, and rely on His grace; cf. pp. 169, 170; Visual Aid 22.)

In what ways does a Christian mature in victorious living? (See pp. 171, 172; Chalkboard 23.) *What common "building blocks" does each of these steps have?* (The twin, and inseparable, virtues of love and obedience.) Close by singing "Faith is the Victory."

Conducting the Class—Plan D

Plan W is especially adaptable, this session, for groups that meet daily or for other reasons do not have time to do much outside reading or preparation. Divide into four groups, or sets of groups, as suggested above, but allow 25 minutes for reading and small group sharing.

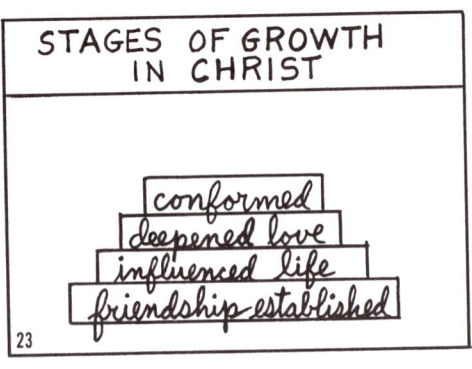

Chalkboard 23

Four general stages of Christian growth (cf. Chalkboard 21 for areas of growth) may be visualized in the form of a pyramid as shown.

SESSION **10**

What Do You Know for Sure? / Text, Chapter 10

Session Goals

The emphasis of this session, as the title clearly implies, is certainty of religious knowledge. It is a recurring theme in this epistle, but has not been stressed in the *Text* until this lesson. Keep in mind, as discussed in Session 8 (*Text,* p. 140), that spiritual knowledge means more than having the facts of right doctrine—it includes a right relationship with God. First John 5:6-21 focuses on what some of the most important of these certainties are and on how a Christian can know them "for sure." Your goal should be to increase the confidence of your members in these truths and to help them allow this assurance to strengthen their faithfulness to the Lord.

Preparation

Since few, if any, of your members will need to be convinced about the basic truths discussed, concentrate on ways to help them convert truth into living. As you prepare, be on the lookout for practical ideas for applying the truths of these doctrines to daily life. The last three discussed in the *Text* are rich in practical relevance, and some suggestions are given in Plan W. But your own discoveries of application, and the discoveries of your class members, will be by far more significant. Especially if this will be the last session of the course, determine that by the Spirit's help your study will result in changed lives—lives that are more real.

Conducting the Class—Plan W

After prayer, ask, *Is it presumptuous, as some charge, for a Christian ever to say, "I know with absolute certainty . . ."?* (Depends, of course, on what is asserted. Many Christians speak presumptuously about matters on which Scripture is silent or unclear. But where a truth is plainly taught in the Bible, it is presumptuous for a Christian to speak of it in any way but in certainty. Cf. p. 173, par., "The life that is real.")

Use Chalkboard 24 as a discussion guide. Add the five "certainties" as they are dealt with, discussing also, if time permits, some of the popular misconceptions regarding each.

Unless you have some skeptics in the class, discuss the first two certainties briefly—not, of course, because they are not important (they are the *most* important), but because, as mentioned under *Preparation* above, your members are already convinced of them. In relation to the general topic of belief, ask, *In the broadest sense, is there such a thing as a completely faithless person?* (No, because everyone has faith in something; cf. p. 173.) *What is always meant in Scripture by faithlessness?* (Lack of trust in God and in His Word, and failure to obey Him.)

[ASK] *What three conditions must believers meet before they can expect God to answer their prayers?* (Confess known sin, pray in God's will, and claim His promises. Cf. 1 John 3:21, 22; 5:15; Matt. 6:10; *Text*, pp. 178-180. In discussing claiming of God's promises, you may want to refer to Visual Aid 22 in the last session.) [ASK] *If God already knows our needs better than we do and wants to fulfill them, why do we need to pray about them?* (One purpose of prayer is that believers consciously express their desires to their heavenly Father as evidence of their dependence and reliance on Him; cf. p. 179.) *What are some dangers in prayer?* (True prayer has *no* dangers. False prayer has many pitfalls, however, among which are a type of "self-hypnosis" in which we talk ourselves into a given attitude or course of action, confusing a good feeling with answered prayer and a bad feeling with unanswered, or using prayer to impress others of our piety; etc. Cf. p. 181.)

The difference between habitual/practiced sin and occasional sin was discussed in Session 6. It is the former kind that is mentioned in 5:18. At this time focus on how Satan, through the flesh and the world, leads a Christian into sin and how Christ will keep us from sinning. Ask, [ASK] *Can Satan, entirely on his own, make a Christian sin?* (No, he must have the person's consent—which is usually given piece-

---

CENTRAL CERTAINTIES
1- Jesus is God
   witness—water, blood, spirit
2- Eternal life through faith in Christ
3- God answers prayer
4- Christians don't practice sin
5- Christian life is only real life

24

Chalkboard 24
These five certainties are basic elements of one of the epistle's three major themes—truth (light). See Chalkboard 3.

meal, starting with minor and increasing to major concessions; cf. p. 182.) *Can a believer keep himself from sinning?* (As anyone familiar with the Bible as a whole, or even with the rest of 1 John, should suspect, the Authorized translation of 5:18, "keepeth himself," is misleading. Only Christ can keep us from sin; cf. p.183, 2 pars. "Then how does.") *Obviously sin is never "good," but is a Christian's sin really so damaging, since it's "covered by the blood of Jesus"?* (Some Christians seem to think it's not, but this betrays the worst sort of presumption and ignorance of God's Word. See *Text*, pp. 184, 185, beginning "When a believer sins.")

Have a class member read 1 John 5:20 from the Phillips translation (it is printed in the *Text*, p. 186). This is obviously the key verse for the entire study, *Be Real. Does this verse mean that a Christian's living is always real?* (No. It could be put that our *life* is real—we irrevocably have God's new and real nature—but our *living*—the way we "live our lives"—can easily slip into unreality, which is any sort of living apart from God's will; cf. p. 187 ff.) If time permits, use Chalkboard 25 as a guide for discussing some of the unreal, idolatrous ideals and practices a Christian may follow.

Make sure you end on a positive note. Ask members to share specific ways they will try to increase fellowship with the Lord and more obediently follow His Word—the twofold secret of the life that is real. List these on the board as they are suggested. This will not only help make the suggestions specific but can serve as a prayer list to follow as you close the session (and possibly the course).

Conducting the Class—Plan D

Divide into groups to study the last three sections of the chapter, pages 178-190. Use Chalkboard 24 and questions from Plan W to help guide discussion.

Chalkboard 25
If you have time to discuss some of the modern idols (spiritual "unrealities"), list them on the board as suggested here. The list is obviously not complete.

POPULAR IDOLS

money — false security
position — false importance
knowledge — false power
health — false welfare
society — false allegiance

25

SESSION **11**

Review Lesson

Session Goals

In this session you may either review the entire course or spend time on one or more subjects that you did not have opportunity to discuss adequately in previous sessions. In some respects this session, to be meaningful, will require more careful preparation than the others. Review is not simply repetition or rehash. It should have two main purposes: to highlight ideas of particular importance or that are still unclear, and to show the entire course in perspective. The latter is especially important when subject areas are somewhat diverse and repeated, as in 1 John.

Preparation

Following are a few suggestions for planning the session. These are necessarily general. Your own plans should be specific, based on your own goals for this session and for the course as a whole.

1 Plan to ask several discussion questions on each lesson. You may want to frame your own or adapt from the "W" lesson plans.

2 Plan to ask questions concerning three or four lessons that were of special interest to your class or on which you think additional study will be helpful.

3 Plan to ask for personal testimonies from class members about how the course has been of value to them. Hopefully some will be able to report ways in which their own lives have become more "real."

Conducting the Class

After prayer, ask for questions or comments from members about any aspect of the course. Unless there is considerable interest, however, allow no more than 10 minutes or so for this.

The following questions are given only as guides. The ones you use should relate to what has been emphasized in class.

● What is the difference between committing and practicing sin, as discussed in the *Text*? Of which can a Christian not be guilty? Why?

● How can and should a Christian benefit from the Bible's honest teaching about believers who sin? Does a Christian *have* to sin?

- In what way is Christian love above the Law? In what way is it not? In what important way is *agape* love different from and above emotion or feeling? Why is Christian love not "blind"? How is Christian love generated?
- What is the love that God hates? What different meanings for "world" are used in Scripture? How is the term used in 1 John? Does worldliness necessarily involve moral sin?
- Of what value is sincerity alone as far as the truthfulness of what we believe is concerned? Why is Satan an imitator and counterfeiter? What are a Christian's main protections against false teaching? Why is a balanced understanding of *all* of God's Word so important?
- In light of what great future event does the Bible frequently admonish us to holy living? How and why is a Christian's sin worse than that of an unbeliever? What two great works of Christ on the cross are mentioned in 1 John 3?
- Assuming they are not expressed in action, who suffers most from such sins as lust, hatred, and covetousness? Why is indifference to the needs of others such a common and dangerous sin—even among Christians? In what ways are the costs of salvation and of discipleship alike and in what way are they different?
- What are some common misinterpretations concerning the biblical truth that God is love? What does the Bible mean by the term, "knowing God"? Why must Christian love, to be complete and effective, involve the mind and the will? Why must love determine not only what we do but how we do it? How can being "nice" sometimes be no indication of love?
- What kind of fear does love include? What kind does love exclude? Why is honesty invigorating and hypocrisy debilitating? In what way are Christians often not victorious? What is the greatest barrier to victorious Christian living?
- When is it presumptuous and when is it not presumptuous for a Christian to claim absolute certainty? When is it presumptuous *not* to claim certainty? If God knows our needs better than we do and wants to meet them, why do we need to pray about them? Can Satan make a Christian sin? What is the difference between real *life* and real *living,* as far as Christians are concerned? About which should a Christian be more concerned?

SESSION **12**

Examination / Optional

The examination may be used for an entire session or part of a session, or it may be omitted altogether. In place of a test, you may prefer to continue the review from last session or spend the time in deeper study of an especially interesting or important area.

Since assignments, lecture, discussion, and general class makeup vary so greatly, it is far better for the teacher to decide on the specific type and length of questions. You will want the examination to cover primarily what has been emphasized in class.

You may want to have members write essays or general observations about one of the problem areas studied. If so, let them know about it well ahead of time so they can plan what they will write. Since this will not be a graded test, advance preparation is not only permissible, but desirable. Such a project could help greatly in a student's clarifying his own ideas. Hopefully his knowledge, attitudes, and motivations concerning family living will have improved during, and because of, this course. You could, in fact, encourage class members to mention ways in which they feel the course has helped them.

If you choose to give a question and answer test, questions found throughout the *Guide* should be helpful. Allow at least 20 minutes after the test for members to share and discuss answers. The purpose of the test should not be so much to determine factual knowledge, or opinions, as to increase and clarify understanding.